Moder
Archit

Series - 2

Glass Buildings

TABLE OF CONTENTS

1- Jacob K Javits Conve|nsion Center

The Jacob K. Javits Convention Center, commonly known as the Javits Center, is a large convention center located on Eleventh Avenue, between 34th and 40th streets, in Hell's Kitchen, Manhattan, New York City. It was designed by architect James Ingo Freed of Pei Cobb Freed & Partners.

Address: 429 11th Ave, New York, NY 10001, United States

Owner: Empire State Development Corporation

Parking: Pay parking nearby

Architects: James Ingo Freed, Richard Rogers

Comment:

The whole building is steel structure and blue glass with its transparent look especially when lit at night, the perfect workmanship and attention to details, makes it a wonderful design.

Interior view – enormous amount of steel

2- Louvre Pyramid

The Louvre Pyramid is a large glass and metal pyramid designed by Chinese-American architect I. M. Pei, surrounded by three smaller pyramids, in the main courtyard of the Louvre Palace in Paris. The large pyramid serves as the main entrance to the Louvre Museum.

Address: 75001 Paris, France

Height: 21 m

Opened: April 1, 1989

Architect: I. M. Pei

Architectural styles: Modern architecture, Futurist architecture

3- The Glass House

Carlo Santambrogio and Ennio Arosio pursue and achieve their design intention in which glass figures as the unquestioned protagonist, excluding the mediation of supports that would challenge its leading role. "That image is symbolic," they comment. "We're portrayed standing on a transparent sheet of glass. We're on the upper floor of the Milan showroom, in reality absorbed into a dimension which effaces every distinction between spaces and relates the interior to the setting outside, the urban context. So often, at least virtually, the boundary line vanishes, and we receive the impression of an unbroken vision".

Comment:
The only issue with this design is there is no privacy unless the owners add curtains in bedrooms and bathrooms to be conservative. The other issue is that glass staircase and floors are slippery needs treatment specially when wet cleaning all this glass is also an issue.

Glass bed and floors

Glass furniture

Glass Staircase and glass floors

4- Glass Graham House By E. Cobb Architects

Multiple floors, patios and a view at every angle, this glass house is a gorgeous piece of architecture come to life. Designed by Seattle-based studio E. Cobb Architects.

Cobb Architects has designed the **Graham Residence**. Located in Mercer Island, Washington, This amazing contemporary **house** was completed in 2010.

Comment:

Fantastic design with beautiful details mixing steel and wood interiors, very classy.

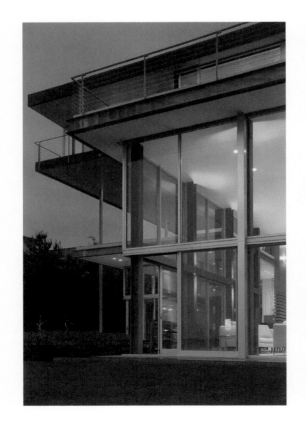

5- The Glass Pavilion, an ultramodern house by Steve Hermann

Known for his modern designs, Los-Angeles-based architect **Steve Hermann** has completed The Glass Pavilion in 2010.

Located on a three-and-a-half acres lot in Santa Barbara, California, the 13,875 square foot luxury home features five bedrooms, five-and-a-half bathrooms, a kitchen with a wine room and an art gallery that displays the architect's vintage car collection.

The architect originally built the home for himself, but changed his plans and put the residence on the market last year for $35,000,000, cars and furniture not included!

Comment:

Beautiful white and black contrast touch in interior design with spaces open to the landscape gardens makes this house a stunning place to live in.

6- Red Hill Residence by David Luck Architecture

South Yarra-based studio **David Luck Architecture** has designed the Red Hill Residence project. Completed in 2002, this nice contemporary weekend retreat is located on the Victorian Mornington Peninsula, a peninsula located south-east of Melbourne in Victoria, Australia.

This glass skin is punctured by a steel bridge that leads into the main room, twisted on axis to true north and on axis back to the central city of Melbourne. Window openings on this room are on all the cardinal points. Views to the Bay and Melbourne are forfeited so one turns back – inward. Lookout house emphasis becomes of the self and not one of external entertainment.

7- Lake Side Studio, California

The modern interior design is not only the main character of **House** MV. You can see another interesting character design in its outdoor living area. House overlooking the American River The house is a combination of flexible living space, art **studio** and gallery. It provides ... **Lakeside Studio** by Mark Dziewulski Architect, **California.**

8- Amazon's Seattle Giant Biospheres

The **Amazon** Spheres are three spherical conservatories that comprise part of the **Amazon** headquarters campus in Seattle, Washington, United States. **Designed** by NBBJ and landscape firm Site Workshop, the three glass domes ... The spheres were dedicated on January 29, 2018, by **Jeff Bezos**

Workers are entering a new phase of construction at Amazon's new campus on the edge of downtown Seattle, beginning the installation of glass panels on the exterior of the massive biospheres that are destined to become an icon of the technology giant's expansion in its booming hometown.

9- Oving Architecten envelopes former concentration camp house in glass box

This touching, yet jarring memorial to Holocaust victims designed by Dutch studio Oving Architecten encloses the former home of an SS Nazi officer in a giant glass box. One of the last remaining structures in the former Kamp Westerbork, the house will now be used as an educational center.

According to the architects, the steel and glass shroud around the home acts as a memorial, conveying the immense human suffering that took place on site, "The spatial approach was to stage the human scale and the relation with the landscape. The project is positioned along the main access to the camp – the Boulevard des Miseres – and you enter it by walking through a low and closed part which facilitates pantry, toilets and storage," they added. "This is also thought as a transition before you reach the glass cover."

Read on for more details about this unique exhibit

https://inhabitat.com/oving-architecten-envelopes-former-concentration-camp-house-in-glass-box/

ABOUT THE AUTHOR

Lamya Sabah is an architect with over 20 years of experience in architectural design and shop drawings production. Master's degree in architecture from The University of Auckland in New Zealand in May 2000. Has worked on large projects with professional architectural consultants, project management firms and contractors in several international cities.
Interested in research and collecting information in related subjects such as design - interior design, home & garden and landscape.

REFRENCES

Javits Center
https://javitscenter.com/about/

Pei Cobb Freed & Partners
https://www.pcf-p.com/projects/jacob-k-javits-convention-center-and-plaza/

TVS Design
https://www.tvsdesign.com/portfolio-posts/jacob-k-javits-convention-center/

Santambrogio Milano – All Glass Design and Architecture
https://www.santambrogiomilano.com/the-glass-house

https://www.santambrogiomilano.com/realizations

TREDIR
https://www.trendir.com/stunning-modern-glass-houses/

Home Design

https://www.homedsgn.com/2011/07/16/graham-house-by-e-cobb-architects/

https://www.homedsgn.com/2011/03/30/the-glass-pavilion-an-ultramodern-house-by-steve-hermann/

https://www.homedsgn.com/2012/01/09/red-hill-residence-by-david-luck-architecture/

Architecture and Design
https://www.architecturendesign.net/graham-house-by-e-cobb-architects/

Mark Dziewulski Architects
http://www.dzarchitect.com/projects.php?projects_id=2

Geek Wire
https://www.geekwire.com/2016/amazons-giant-seattle-spheres/

Inhabitat
https://inhabitat.com/oving-architecten-envelopes-former-concentration-camp-house-in-glass-box/westerbork-oving-architecten-2/